SPORTS SCIENCE

Swimming

Hélène Boudreau

W
FRANKLIN WATTS
LONDON•SYDNEY

This edition first published in 2009
by Franklin Watts

Copyright © 2009
The Brown Reference Group Ltd

Franklin Watts
338 Euston Road
London NW1 3BH

Franklin Watts Australia
Level 17/207 Kent Street
Sydney, NSW 2000

A CIP catalogue record for this book is available
from the British Library.

Dewey no: 797.2

ISBN 978 0 7496 8669 7

Printed in China

Franklin Watts is a division of Hachette Children's Books,
an Hachette UK company.
www.hachette.co.uk

Note to parents and teachers concerning websites:
In the book every effort has been made by the Publishers to
ensure that websites are suitable for children, that they are
of the highest educational value, and that they contain no
inappropriate or offensive material. However, because of the
nature of the Internet, it is impossible to guarantee that the
contents of these sites will not be altered. We advise that
Internet access is supervised by a responsible adult.

For The Brown Reference Group plc:
Designer: Lynne Lennon
Picture Researcher: Sean Hannaway
Editor: Leon Gray
Managing Editor: Tim Cooke
Art Director: Jeni Child
Design Manager: David Poole
Editorial Director: Lindsey Lowe
Children's Publisher: Anne O'Daly

Every effort has been made to trace the owners
of copyrighted material.

Photo credits

Front cover: Vasily Smirnov/Shutterstock
Backgrounds: Gert Johannes Jacobus Vrey/Shutterstock

Action Images: Paulo Santos 5t, Christophe Launay 5b, CSPA
6–7, Jim Young 9t, Christinne Muschi 14–15, 21t, 24–25,
Stephane Kempinaire 15, 18l, 18r, 19bl, 19br, Vincent Kessler
17t, Brent Smith 19t, David Callow 20, MDB 21b, Gustau
Nacarino 22, Wolfgang Rattay 23t, Philippe Millereau 23b, Jeff
Haynes 25t, Nigel Roddis 25b, Kimimasa Mayama 26, Sporting
Pictures 27b; Ansys Inc: 29b; Corbis: Bettmann 13b, Ted Levine
16; Getty Images: Al Bello 4, Timothy A. Clary 7t, Martin
Bernetti 7b, Daniel Berehulak 8, Quinn Rooney 10, Jose Luis
Roca 11tl, Greg Wood 12–13, Donald Miralle 14, Adam Pretty
27t; PA Photos: Anders Wiklund 17b, Chris Ison 28, Luis M.
Alvarez 29t; Shutterstock: Yana Petruseva 11cr, AGphotographer
11cr, Regien Paassen 11cr, Filip Fuxa 11cr

Illustrations: Mark Walker 12

Contents

Introducing Swimming

Cave paintings from more than 6,000 years ago show that people have been swimming since prehistoric times. Through the ages, people swam to travel across bays, lakes and rivers. They also swam to fish for food and for fun.

Swimming as a sport began in England in the 1800s. Competitive swimming appeared at the first modern Olympic Games in Athens in 1896. Swimmers were dropped into the icy waters of the Mediterranean Sea.

Outdoor pools are popular in places where the climate is hot and dry.

FACT! ▶▶▶▶▶▶▶

Different strokes

FINA has approved four strokes for competitive swimming races. They are the front crawl (or freestyle), breaststroke, backstroke and butterfly.

NEW WORDS

FINA: The Fédération Internationale de Natation is the world governing body for swimming competitions.

LOOK CLOSER

Amazon Swim 2007

Martin Strel of Slovenia (pictured right) was tired on 7 April, 2007. That day he finished his 5,268-kilometre (3,270-mile) swim along the Amazon River – the longest river in the world. Strel swam for 10 hours a day for 66 days to make his trip. He's been nicknamed 'Daredevil', 'Fishman' and 'The Craziest Man in the World'.

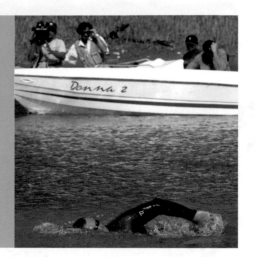

The first swimmer to reach the shore was the winner. At first, only men were allowed to compete. Women started to compete in 1912. Most swimming races take place in swimming pools. The swimmers compete in different swimming styles over different distances. However, some swimming competitions still take place in open water, such as rivers, lakes and the open ocean.

Energy gels and sports drinks help to fuel swimmers' bodies. Scientists and coaches study swimmers' techniques with video cameras and **wind tunnels** to help them swim faster. These are just some examples of how science has changed the sport of swimming.

Some races take place in oceans. Swimmers follow a course marked by buoys.

Swim science

Science plays a big role as swimming becomes more competitive. High-tech body suits help to lower drag force as swimmers glide through the water.

Wind tunnel: A chamber used to study how fluids flow over different objects.

Pool Science

There is more to a swimming pool than just a hole in the ground. In fact, a lot of science goes into designing and maintaining a swimming pool. Competitive swimming takes place in an Olympic-size pool.

Swimming pools are divided into lanes for competitive races.

Olympic pools follow size rules. They must be 25 metres (82 feet) wide, 50 metres (164 feet) long and 2 metres (6½ feet) deep. The walls of the pool must be strong enough to take the pressure of 2.5 million litres (5.3 million pints) of water. Modern pools are designed to help swimmers. Specially designed lane markers reduce **turbulence**. Pool gutters absorb waves.

Cleaning with chlorine

With many swimmers a day, the water needs to be kept clean and free of germs. Chlorine is a cheap and easy way to keep the water in a pool clean. The chlorine forms two chemicals when it dissolves in water. Hydrochloric acid kills bacteria quickly. Chloric acid kill bacteria slowly. It also fades the colour from swimsuits.

NEW WORDS

Turbulence: The irregular flow of water.

LOOK CLOSER

What's that smell?

Swimmers leave skin cells, mucous and dirt in the pool. These are sources of nitrogen. Chlorine reacts with nitrogen to keep the water clean. This happens in a chemical cycle. If there is not enough chlorine, the cycle can stop in the **trichloramine** stage. Trichloramines are what most people think of as the smell in the pool. Adding more chlorine to complete the chemical cycle gets rid of the smell.

Regularly cleaning the pool removes sources of organic nitrogen, such as skin cells.

That's why it is important to rinse suits under water after a dip in a chlorinated pool. Some people think that the strong smell in a swimming pool means that too much chlorine has been added to the water. In fact, it is lack of chlorine that causes the smell.

San Alfonso del Mar in Chile is home to the world's largest swimming pool.

►►►►►►►► FACT!
Chile pool

The world's biggest swimming pool is at a holiday resort in San Alfonso del Mar, Chile. It is 1 kilometre (⅝ mile) long – that's almost as long as ten football pitches. It holds about 6,000 times more water than an Olympic-size pool.

Trichloramine: A chemical that is produced when chlorine reacts with nitrogen.

Swimming Gear

Swimming gear is pretty simple. The essential items are a swimsuit and a towel – what could be easier?

Other basic equipment includes a swimming cap to keep the hair out of the water. Some swimmers also use goggles, ear plugs or nose plugs to keep water out of their eyes, ears and nose.

Training gear

Swimmers use a range of training gear to improve and get faster. They keep track of swim times, both in training and in competition, using stopwatches. Flutter boards, floats and pull buoys help to improve stroke technique and kicking strength. Swimmers use weights and other gym equipment to strengthen and stretch their muscles.

Most swimmers wear goggles to protect the eyes and a swimming hat to keep the hair dry.

NEW WORDS

Drag: The slowing force on a swimmer as he or she moves through the water.

Swimmers use a range of training aids in the pool.

▶ ▶ ▶ ▶ ▶ ▶ ▶ ▶

FACT!

Record breakers

Many world records have been broken in recent years by swimmers wearing new high-tech swimsuits. Some critics say that the suits give swimmers an unfair lead. They argue that it is similar to allowing flippers while racing.

High-tech swimming

As swimming gets more competitive, the gear is getting more high-tech. Scientists have turned to swimsuit technology to help swimmers get faster. Swimmers are constantly fighting against the forces of the water. Some shave their entire bodies to help them slip through the water with less **drag**. New swimsuits are designed to reduce drag. Others help improve muscle performance.

Speedo's Fastskin suit has tiny V-shaped ridges to reduce drag.

LOOK CLOSER

Skinsuits

Speedo's Fastskin suit mimics shark skin. The **hydrodynamic** design of the suit reduces drag. The Adidas Fullbody suit compresses muscles to keep them from getting tired. Arena's Powerskin suit is made of a water-repellent material. Less water gets absorbed in the suit, which makes it lighter. The new Speedo LZR Racer swimsuit is out of this world. Researchers used a NASA wind tunnel, as well as 400 body scans of athletes, to help develop the suit.

Hydrodynamic: The flow of water around an object.

Food for Fuel

Swimming training and competitive races use up a lot of energy. Swimmers use muscles in their arms, legs and torsos. Swimming also takes concentration to maintain stroke technique and breathing and time perfect turns.

It is important to drink lots of fluid during training.

The body's muscles and brain need a steady supply of energy to work at peak performance. Swimmers must fuel their bodies with a healthy balance of **carbohydrates**, protein, fats, vitamins and minerals. All these nutrients are found in different foods and drinks.

Food for thought

Cereal grains and fresh fruits and vegetables are good sources of carbohydrates. They provide quick energy for explosive starts and sprint finishes. Protein comes from eggs, lean meats and nuts. It helps to build and repair muscles. Fats from oils store

NEW WORDS

Carbohydrates: Substances in food made from carbon, hydrogen and oxygen.

Long-distance swimmers need to eat to boost energy supplies.

energy. This store of body fuel is good for long races. To pack in fast calories between meals, some swimmers turn to energy bars or gels. These quick sources of energy are made up of complex carbohydrates, protein, vitamins and minerals.

Take a drink

Swimmers sweat just like any athlete. Even though they are surrounded by water, they can become dehydrated. Water will quench thirst, but sports drinks are a better choice. These drinks are specially made to replace lost fluids and **electrolytes** in the body.

▶ ▶ ▶ ▶ ▶ ▶ ▶ ▶

FACT!

Calorie calculator

Competitive swimmers can use up to 5,000 calories during workouts. An average-size man needs about 2,500 calories a day for regular activity.

Swimmers should eat a range of different foods to stay healthy.

LOOK CLOSER

Calorie count

Carbohydrates, fats and protein are broken down in the body. They react with oxygen to release energy. This energy is measured in calories. One gram of protein or carbohydrate has 4 calories. One gram of fat has 9 calories. A take-away hamburger has up to 700 calories: enough energy to swim for one hour.

Electrolyte: Salt is an example of an electrolyte. It breaks up into charged ions when it dissolves in water.

Water Forces

Swimmers work with and against the forces of the water each time they train or compete.

Buoyancy is the upwards force of water on a swimmer's body. This force helps to keep swimmers afloat. The opposite, downwards force of gravity pulls a swimmer down. Gravity is caused by the pull of the Earth on objects. **Buoyancy** and gravity work against each other. If the force of buoyancy is greater than the force of gravity, a swimmer will float.

Drag slows a swimmer down. Water is 700 times more dense than air and provides more resistance. That's why wading knee deep in water is much harder than walking on the beach.

There are four forces at work when you swim at the surface of the water.

buoyancy

drag

thrust

gravity

NEW WORDS

Thrust: The forwards force created by the movement of a swimmer's arms and legs.

Fighting forces

Gravity acts through the body's centre of gravity, which usually lies between the swimmer's hips and belly button. The lower part of the body is denser (bones and muscles of the legs) than the top half (lungs, arms and head). The centre of buoyancy is usually a

The same four forces are acting on this swimmer as she stretches out under the water.

LOOK CLOSER

Floating facts

A swimmer will float depending on where the centre of gravity and centre of buoyancy are on his or her body. The centre of buoyancy and the centre of gravity are closer together in children. So the body of a child stays flatter in the water and floating is easier.

little higher. It is the average position of the buoyant force acting on the body. As swimmers float, gravity pulls down through the centre of gravity. Buoyancy forces push up through the centre of buoyancy. So the lower part of the body hangs down in the water, while the upper body stays afloat.

FACT! Eureka

Archimedes was a Greek mathematician. About 2,000 years ago, he found out how buoyancy forces worked. He realised that if two objects are the same mass, the one with the larger volume floats better.

Buoyancy: The upward force of the water that pushes on a swimmer in the pool.

Cutting through the Water

A swimmer stretches his body to stay streamlined. This helps to cut down drag.

A swimmer swims from start to finish as quickly as possible. He or she aims for maximum **propulsion** and minimum drag.

Swimmers can improve their speed in a few ways. Strong, powerful muscles in the arms, legs and torso aid propulsion. But a lot of this power is wasted if the swimmer has poor stroke technique.

Reducing drag

All moving objects experience drag force as they move through air or water. Water is denser than air, so a swimmer needs to work harder to overcome the resistance of the water. Swimmers can reduce drag when diving in the pool or pushing off the wall by **streamlining**. This means holding the body flat and long, with the arms in front and legs tucked together.

NEW WORDS

Propulsion: The force that drives a swimmer forwards. Propulsion is created by the swimmer's arms and legs.

Efficient stroke technique is the key to fast swimming.

Kicking the legs keeps them in line with the rest of the body. An angled hand position during the stroke helps to produce lift. Stretching with each stroke keeps the body streamlined. All these techniques help to reduce the force of drag.

A swimmer catches his breath in the bow wave created by his head.

LOOK CLOSER

Different types of drag

Frictional drag: Water molecules absorb energy as they bounce off the swimmer's body. This drag is like the resistance you feel when you rub your hand against sandpaper.

Pressure drag: Water builds up in front of the swimmer as he or she speeds through the water. High pressure builds up at the head. The pressure at the feet is lower. The pressure difference causes a sucking force at the feet.

Wave drag: Swimming creates waves around the body. At a certain speed, the wave length is equal to the length of the swimmer's body. This wave drag slows down the swimmer. If the swimmer tries to swim out of line, wave drag gets worse. This limits the top speed a swimmer can reach.

Streamlining: Making the body flat and long to cut through the water with minimum drag.

Fit to Swim

ike all athletes, swimmers need to warm up and stretch before training sessions or races.

A ten-minute warm up of easy swimming boosts blood flow to the muscles. After the warm-up, stretching the shoulders, back, chest, legs and arms reduces the risk of injuries. Each stretch should be done two or three times and held for between 15 and 30 seconds.

⬆ *It is important to warm up before an important race.*

FACT!

▶▶▶▶▶▶▶▶

Ian Thorpe

Ian Thorpe is an Australian Olympic gold medal swimmer. Thorpe trained 35 hours a week to get in shape. He swam up to 120 kilometres (75 miles) each week.

Sets and drills

Swimmers run through a series of drills to perfect stroke technique. Each drill focuses on one part of the stroke at a time. An example is a front crawl drill called 'catch-up'. During the drill, swimmers only do arm pulls. They

NEW WORDS

Cross training: Keeping fit by training in sports other than swimming.

Stretching keeps the muscles supple and ready for competition.

LOOK CLOSER

Cross training

Swimmers do more than just swim to keep in top shape. **Cross training** helps to build a strong, balanced body. This helps prevent injuries. Strength training in the gym helps tone muscles that might not be used regularly in swimming. Running helps build **endurance** for long swim races. Cross training is also a great way to keep training interesting.

concentrate on one side of the body at a time. By repeating the movement over and over, the muscles 'remember' the swimming movement until it becomes automatic. A series of drills focusing on different parts of the stroke is called a set. Sets help swimmers perfect their stroke technique and swim stronger.

Brain training

A swimmer's brain must also be ready for the race. Competitive swimmers use visualisation to help them perform to their best ability. They prepare their minds by thinking through starts, turns and stroke rate. Running through the race, step-by-step, helps to focus the mind better on race day.

Swimming aids, such as paddles, help to improve stroke technique.

Endurance: A measure of an athlete's ability to keep on exercising.

Stroke Science Crawl

The front crawl, or freestyle, is the most common swimming stroke. It is also the fastest. Each part of the stroke and kick is to drive the swimmer forward and overcome the forces of drag.

LOOK CLOSER

Newton's third law

In the third law of motion, Sir Isaac **Newton** states that for every action there is an equal and opposite reaction. Pulling the water back during the crawl pushes the body forward.

During the pull, the hand pulls water from the front to the back of the body. Originally, swimmers brought the hand straight back through the water during the pull. But this technique wastes a lot of energy and

The propulsive force of the crawl comes from the arms. One arm pulls while the other recovers.

NEW WORDS

Newton: English scientist Sir Isaac Newton (1643-1727) came up with the three laws of motion.

FACT!

▶ ▶ ▶ ▶ ▶ ▶ ▶ ▶ ▶

Record breaker

In 2007, American swimmer Kate Ziegler shaved more than nine seconds off the 1,500-m (0.9 mile) freestyle world record, with a time of 15 minutes and 42 seconds.

creates drag. A more efficient pull uses an angled hand through the water. Also, using an S-type movement, called **sculling**, lets the hand come in contact with more water. This increases the power of the pull.

Recovery

While one arm is pulling, the other is recovering and preparing for the next stroke. Extending the hand as much as possible with each stroke lengthens the body and reduces wave drag.

Breathing

The swimmer takes a breath every two or three strokes. Sighting the bottom of the pool between breaths ensures the swimmer is going in a straight line.

The kick

The **flutter kick** (see page 22) helps to balance the body in the water. The legs kick to help keep the body flat and reduce drag. The kick also provides some propulsive forces, but not as much as the arm pulls.

Sculling: Moving the hands in a S-shape through the water to increase the power of the pull.

Stroke Science Breaststroke

The breaststroke is one of the slowest swimming strokes. But that does not mean it is the easiest. It takes a lot of practice to time the arm pull, whip kick, and breathing into one fluid stroke.

The breaststroke is done on the front. To start, the palms are together at the chest. The legs are straight and together. The legs then whip kick similar to the way in which a frog kicks. This forces the body forward. The arms reach to the front in a glide as the legs come back together. The arms then pull the water back. The hands are tilted at an angle and move in an outward, then inward, sculling motion. The palms come back together at the chest. The face comes out of the water to take a breath. This completes one cycle of the stroke.

➡ *Swimmers need to work on their technique to master the breaststroke.*

NEW WORDS

Tumble turns: Flip turns used to change directions when approaching the wall of the pool.

LOOK CLOSER

Kicking power

In the breaststroke, the swimmer gets most power from the whip kick. The arm stroke drives the body forward, too, but its main job is to let the swimmer take a breath and get the body back into position for the next kick.

⬇ **The whip kick provides about 70 per cent of the breaststroke's power.**

Breaststroke rules

Freestyle and butterfly swimmers do **tumble turns** to change directions at the end of the lane. Breaststroke swimmers do 'open turns'. They touch the wall with both hands and rotate to push off with their feet. Swimmers must be belly down as they push off. They are allowed one **dolphin kick** while streamlining before their first stroke. When finishing the race, they must also touch the wall with both hands.

▶ ▶ ▶ ▶ ▶ ▶ ▶ ▶ ▶

FACT! Liesel Jones

Australian Liesel Jones (pictured left) was 15 when she took silver in the 100 metre (333 ft) breaststroke at the 2000 Sydney Olympics. This made her the youngest ever Olympic swimming medallist.

Dolphin kick: An undulating kick in which the legs are held together and move up and down.

Stroke Science Backstroke

As its names suggests, the backstroke, or back crawl, is swum on the back. The arms take turns pulling water, while the legs flutter kick to aid propulsion.

At the start and at turns, backstroke swimmers glide under the water.

To start the backstroke, one hand comes out of the water, thumb first, near the hip. The shoulder and hip rotate up as the arm windmills and reaches above the head. The hand then enters the water above the head, smallest finger first, to start the underwater pull. The arm draws through the water in a sculling motion, similar to a backward front crawl. While one arm is pulling, the other is recovering.

Body rotation

Rotating the body with each stroke helps in two ways. First, when the body slices through the water on an angle, similar to the V-shape of the bottom of a boat, there is less resistance. Second, tilting the body lets the large torso muscles add power to the stroke.

NEW WORDS

Flutter kick: The most common swimming kick in which the legs move up and down without bending the knees.

Kicking

The **flutter kick** is similar to the one used in front crawl, but it is upside down. It adds a bit of propulsion, but its main job is to keep the legs and body in a straight, streamlined position. This reduces drag.

▶ ▶ ▶ ▶ ▶ ▶ ▶ ▶

FACT!

Natalie Coughlin

American Natalie Coughlin became the first ever woman to break the one minute barrier in the 100 metre (333 ft) backstroke in 2002. She broke her own World Record in 2007 when she swam it in 59.44 seconds.

⬇ *The arm you can see above the water is in the recovery phase of the stroke.*

LOOK CLOSER

Poor technique

Overreaching, leading the stroke with the back of the hand, and entering too wide are common backstroke mistakes. These poor techniques all add drag and slow the swimmer down.

⬆ *To keep the head perfectly still, this backstroke swimmer is balancing a bottle on her head while swimming.*

Backstroke markers

During the backstroke, the head is kept still with the chin tucked in. Flags across the pool show the swimmer that there are only 5 metres (16 ft) left before the wall. That way, the swimmer can prepare for the next turn or a sprint to the finish.

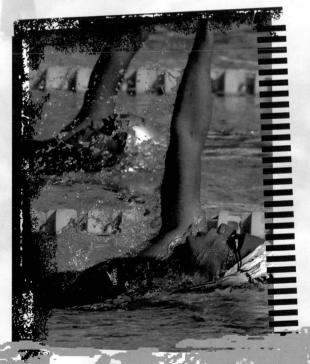

Overreaching: When a swimmer reaches too far with the hand during the stroke.

Stroke Science Butterfly

The butterfly is the hardest swimming stroke to master. It takes a lot of practice to combine the arm pull, dolphin kick, and breathing into a smooth, gliding stroke.

The swimmer starts the stroke in a glide position. The body is straight, with the arms outstretched in front of the body. The face is in the water. To start the first pull, the swimmer bends the legs up at the knee and kicks them both together like a dolphin's tail. Both arms pull through the water to drive the body forward. The pull is similar to the crawl, but both arms pull together.

Stroke sequence

During the recovery phase, the swimmer kicks again to lift the head, arms and upper chest out of the water. The swimmer usually takes a breath every other stroke.

⬆ *As with all swimming strokes, the swimmer breathes in during the recovery and breathes out under the water.*

NEW WORDS

Peak speed: The fastest part of a swimming stroke.

FACT!

▶▶▶▶▶▶▶▶▶

Michael Phelps

American Michael Phelps (pictured right) has broken the 200 metre (666 ft) butterfly World Record six times. He broke his own record at the 2008 Beijing Olympics, where he won eight gold medals in different events.

The hands then enter the water, thumbs first and shoulder width apart, and the swimmer dives forward into the water. A small whip kick keeps the legs from sinking too far down into the water before the next stroke.

Stroke speed

The **peak speed** of the butterfly is quicker than the front crawl, because both arms pull together. It is slower overall, however, because the stroke slows down during the **recovery phase**.

➡ *The butterfly is similar to the front crawl, but both arms pull and recover at the same time.*

LOOK CLOSER

Building the butterfly

Swimming coach David Armbruster invented the butterfly in 1934. He wanted to develop a stroke that would reduce drag and improve the speed of the breaststroke. Armbruster found that by bringing the arms out of the water, swimmers moved faster. One of his swimmers, Jack Sieg, came up with the dolphin kick a year later. They put the stroke and the kick together to create the butterfly.

Recovery phase: The part of the stroke when the swimmer gets ready for the next power phase.

Racing Tactics

Modern Olympic races have 32 events for swimmers. Pool races range from 50 to 1,500 metres (160 to 4,800 ft). There is also a 10-km (6¼-mile) open-water race.

Swim races are won and lost in hundredths of a second. An explosive start is vital. At the first starter's signal, the swimmers take position on the **starting blocks** (or backstroke grips). Their hands reach down to the blocks, one on top of the other.

All the races apart from backstroke start from the starting blocks.

➡️ *A swimmer tumble turns at the end of the lane and drives off the wall to start the next length.*

The swimmers tuck their heads in and curl their toes over the edge of the blocks to help push off. The knees are bent, ready to dive forward when the starting pistol fires. The swimmers then dive into the water and stretch out into a streamlined position to prevent drag.

Tumble turns

Tumble turns are a quick, efficient way for swimmers to change direction at the end of the lane. A compact tuck and streamlined body after the push off helps to reduce drag. It is important for swimmers to stay strong through the middle of the race. If a swimmer does not stay focused, this is where valuable time can be lost.

LOOK CLOSER

Race for the clock

Swimmers tag an electronic touch pad set at the end of each lane when they finish. Touching the pad sends a signal to the timing clock. The finish time is then registered on the scoreboard.

▶▶▶▶▶▶▶

FACT!

Mark Spitz

At the 1972 Olympics, Mark Spitz won seven gold medals. His record lasted until 2008, when Michael Phelps took eight golds. The International Olympic Committee (IOC) chose Spitz as one of its five athletes of the century. Phelps is sure to follow.

NEW WORDS

Starting blocks: Raised platforms on which the swimmers wait for the race to start (apart from backstroke races).

The Future of Swimming

Swimmers, scientists, and personal trainers continue to find new ways to improve pool technology and swimming times. New ideas are sure to keep this exciting sport on the cutting edge of science for years to come.

An endless pool is a miniature version of a normal swimming pool. Swimmers swim against a current in a similar way to a runner moving over the escalator of a treadmill. The pool can be kept small because the swimmer does not really move. The speed of the current can be adjusted to suit the swimmer. An endless pool can move up to 19,000 litres (40,000 pints) of water a minute.

Sports scientists use an endless pool to assess the fitness of a swimmer.

NEW WORDS

Nanotechnology: Technology that involves working with substances at the molecular level.

Swimming in miniature

Nanotechnology is the science of changing matter on an atomic or molecular level. One company is using nanotechnology to treat pool water. Their device uses **crystals** that convert bacteria, skin cells, and other organic waste into carbon dioxide and water. The waste is broken down into simple molecules so there are no solids to be filtered from the pool.

Pool technology

Many pools are now fitted with electronic control systems. A computer monitors the pool water and pumps. If there is a problem, the system adjusts the pool settings automatically. As a result, the owner does not have to spend as much time looking after the pool.

Coaches video swimmers to assess stroke technique.

Computational fluid dynamics is used to map the flow of water around a swimmer's body.

LOOK CLOSER

Computational fluid dynamics (CFD)

CFD uses maths to model and predict the flow of fluids such as water. CFD has been used in the oil industry for years. Sports scientists and coaches are now using it to help train their athletes. An Australian research project is looking for ways to use CFD to help their Olympic swimmers. By studying how water flows past swimmers, coaches can help to find new ways to overcome drag and increase swimming power.

Crystals: Solids consisting of atoms, molecules, or ions held together in a regular, repeating pattern.

Glossary

Buoyancy: The upwards force of the water that pushes on a swimmer in the pool.

Carbohydrates: Substances in food made from carbon, hydrogen and oxygen.

Cross training: Keeping fit by training in sports other than swimming.

Crystals: Solids consisting of atoms, molecules or ions that are held together in a regular, repeating pattern.

Dolphin kick: An undulating kick in which the legs are held together and move up and down.

Drag: The slowing force on a swimmer as he or she moves through the water.

Electrolyte: Salt is an example of an electrolyte. It breaks up into charged ions when it dissolves in water.

Endurance: A measure of an athlete's ability to keep on exercising.

FINA: The Fédération Internationale de Natation is the world governing body for swimming competitions.

Flutter kick: The most common swimming kick, in which the legs move up and down without bending the knees.

Hydrodynamic: The flow of water around an object.

Molecule: The smallest particle of a chemical compound, which is made up of two or more atoms.

Nanotechnology: Technology that involves working with substances at the molecular level.

Newton: English scientist Sir Isaac Newton (1643–1727) came up with the three laws of motion.

Overreaching: When a swimmer reaches too far with his or her hand during the stroke.

Peak speed: The fastest part of the stroke.

Propulsion: The force that drives a swimmer forwards. Propulsion is created by the swimmer's arms and legs.

Recovery phase: The part of the stroke when the swimmer gets ready for the next power phase.

Sculling: Moving the hands in a S-shape through the water to increase the power of the pull.

Starting blocks: Raised platforms on which the swimmers wait for the race to start (apart from backstroke races).

Streamlining: Making the body flat and long to cut through the water with minimum drag.

Trichloramine: A chemical that is produced when chlorine reacts with nitrogen.

Tumble turns: Flip turns used to change directions when approaching the wall of the pool.

Turbulence: The irregular flow of water.

Wind tunnel: A chamber used to study how fluids flow over different objects.

Find Out More

Books

Gifford, Clive. *Swimming (Know Your Sport)*. Franklin Watts, 2008.

Gifford, Clive. *Swimming (Sporting Skills)*. Wayland 2008.

Goodman, Polly. *Exercise and Your Body*. Wayland, 2007.

Hunter, Rebecca. *Swimming (Starting Sport)*. Franklin Watts, 2008.

Storey, Rita. *Swimming (Training to Succeed)*. Franklin Watts, 2009.

Swimming (Know the Game). A&C Black, 2006

Websites

The About.com website explains everything you need to know about swimming. Click on links such as "Psychology & Swim Science" and "Swimming Technique Tips" to find out more detailed information on swimming science and stroke technique.

http://swimming.about.com

This website explores the physics behind swimming — everything from Archimedes' principle to Newton's laws of motion.

http://www.east-buc.k12.ia.us/02_03/CE/km/TP.htm

This self-help guide aims to help nervous swimmers relax in the water. Click on the "Physics" link to find out more about swimming science.

http://www.relaxnswim.com/index.html

Index